heal your relationship with money

Understand your money "why," let go of your past financial dysfunction, and make peace with your money life in just 28 days

By KARA STEVENS

Praise for

heal your relationship with money

"Kara is so awesome! Her work around money and emotions is by far my favorite topic of hers."

--Tiffany "The Budgetnista" Aliche,
New York Times Bestselling Author

Former clients say:

"It hit home for me and really made me understand why I've had such a difficult time with money all my adult life. I'm turning 50 soon and I promised myself life will be different moving forward. I'm healing my financial dysfunction."

-- Carnelius Eldridge

"This information was very much needed. I never actually looked back to understand how and why I think about money the way I do. Eye-opening!"

-- Angela Jackson

KARA STEVENS

"Excellent content. 'Healing Your Relationship with Money' allows you to examine your inner feelings of money, whether it's saving, spending or investing."

-- Mary Doggett

"Thank you so much for doing this course! I love how you shared your personal stories. You taught me to pay closer attention to the way I think about money and to forgive myself and others."

-- Nahomie Johnson

"Excellent and so informing! Searching for the root cause of our behaviors is everything! Only when we have answers can we change for the better, for our best lives! Thank you so much, Kara!"

-- Adia Wilson

"I found 'Heal Your Relationship with Money' so informative. I knew that I needed to reboot my relationship with money, but did not know how to even start. This is a blueprint for creative positive energy - not only with money, but people and circumstances. Loved it!"

-- Hope Elliott

Other Books by Kara Stevens

Unmasking the Strong Black Woman: 16 Essays on How to Manage Your Emotional Health, Build Your Wealth, and Live a Juicy Life (2015)

The Happy Finances Challenge: Learn how to Make Money Decisions that Will Lead to Long-term Financial Happiness is Just 42 days (2018)

WANT MORE SUPPORT?

Want more tools and resources to help you transform how you think and feel about money?

If you're serious about stepping into abundance, breaking cycles, and moving towards a life of bounty and bliss, download your free *Break-Up with Broke Bundle*.

This bundle houses four self-coaching journal prompts and money templates to help you reclaim your financial voice and power.

Carve out a weekend morning at home or at a cafe to do this financial self-care work. You deserve it.

DEDICATION

This book is dedicated to every woman who has ever felt shame about their past and present money decisions. I just want to let you know:

> You were doing the best you could with what you knew.

> You don't have to hide anymore.

> You're not alone.

> You are safe.

> You have the power to transform your finances and your life.

TABLE OF CONTENTS

Introduction 9

Week 1 17

Day 1: Connecting the Dots Between Money and Emotions 17
Day 2: Write the Beginning Chapters of Your Money Story 20
Day 3: Give Your Money a Name and Give it a Voice 23
Day 4: Create a Family Financial Geonogram aka Family Financial Family Tree 27
Day 5: Code and Categorize Your Money Messages 30
Day 6: Draw Some Conclusions 34
Day 7: Forgive with Compassion 38

Week 2 42

Day 8: Silence the Noise 42
Day 9: Build on the Strengths of Your Old Financial Identity 46
Day 10: Embrace Your True Financial Voice or Alter Ego 49
Day 11: Listen to Your Financial Voice or Alter Ego..52
Day 12: Identify Your Core Values 55

Day 13: Align Your Spending to Your Core Values.....59
Day 14: Close the Values Gap..62

Week 3..67

Day 15: Track Your Spending and Saving the Right Way..67
Day 16: Name Your Bank Accounts................................71
Day 17: Schedule Dates with Your Money....................75
Day 18: Assemble Your Money Squad............................78
Day 19: Build Your Money Library.................................82
Day 20: Be a Coin Collector..85
Day 21: Automate Abundance..88

Week 4..91

Day 22: Notice and Name Your Financial Triggers.....91
Day 23: Have a Game Plan for Your Financial Triggers...96
Day 24: Scrutinize Your Money Self-Talk...................100
Day 25: Create a Beautiful Money Space.................... 105
Day 26: Create "Invitation-Only" Statements............ 108
Day 27: Become a Boss at Spotting EF Money......... 114
Day 28: Decide to be Enough Now............................... 117

About the Author 123

Let's Stay Connected 126

INTRODUCTION

When I sat down to write *heal your relationship with money*, so many childhood money memories bubbled to the surface and flooded my thoughts. Some warm and vivid. Others discouraging and disappointing.

My first money memories were the summers I spent in Antigua with my dad and grandparents. My paternal granddad was a cantankerous pharmacist with a high booty, a penchant for high-water bell bottoms independent of style trends, and a deep sense of responsibility and largesse. Every evening my brother and I waited up for him to come home after a long day at the pharmacy.

He would place his tattered brown briefcase full of money on the dining room table, open it, and insist that we help him count the day's earnings. Antiguan money was pretty money, with all types of colors and flourishes for each denomination.

After we successfully counted the money, he broke us each off with a $20 or $50 bill, depending on how generous he was feeling. And even though I was only five or six years old, in those moments, I felt such excitement, joy, power, and pride.

But in between these summer visits to Antigua and my glimpse into the world of Black entrepreneurship and abundance, I lived with my mother, my most powerful financial influence, in America. In Hollis, Queens, a working-class, Black community in New York City, to be exact. My mama, besides being another Antiguan, was also a Black immigrant to the United States with a strong work ethic and British nursing training, determined to snatch up one of those coveted spots in the African-American upper-middle-class echelon.

But when my dad abandoned us to return to Antigua (after she put him through medical school working as a nurse) her world crumpled, and she held on tight to everything she could to salvage her dignity and protect herself, especially her money.

In hindsight, growing up with my mom was an exercise in enduring stretches of emotional and financial deprivation. I loved my mother and she tried her best to train me to be self-sufficient, stoic, educated, and unrelenting. A soldier.

And she was extremely successful with what she set out to do; among the many things I can add to my "things done" list before the age of 35 include: author, Ivy League grad, Fulbright Semi-Finalist, award-winning online business owner, middle school administrator, etc.

But along the way, she taught me some other things about the world through her relationship with money. The various ways she talked about money, stressed about money, felt resentful about her ex-husband and family members about money, taught me, her only doting and obedient daughter, that the world is a scary, scarce place. No matter how hardworking or talented you were or how well you followed the rules, you had no real control over what happened in your life so you should never take risks and always protect your heart.

I learned you had to hold tight to money because nothing was ever guaranteed. I learned you had to protect your money from everyone, especially those close to you. I learned you had to "suck salt" and repress even your simplest desires because survival was the only thing that mattered and happiness was frivolous.

It took years of self-discovery and reflection to realize that my money story was not fully my own; it was an inherited one (and to some degree, my mom's money story wasn't fully hers, either). And it took another set of years to see the beauty in its complexity and nuance. And it took a different set of years to break free and leave all those stories behind and create my own money story.

This book is about the power of naming and rewriting your money story into one that allows you to win emotionally and financially and cultivate a healthy relationship with money. A healthy relationship with money means that your money works for you, rather than against you. You neither hoard it nor squander it. You neither avoid it nor obsess over it. You see it as a tool to create a life of your own choosing.

heal your relationship with money will help you understand your money past, how it relates to your money present, and will equip you with the tools to empower you to rewrite and have ownership of your future financial narrative in a very easy-to-understand way.

In this book, you will receive 28 days of money mindset teachings.

During Week 1, we'll unpack our financial past in order to identify the origins of our current money narrative. During Week 2, we'll focus on silencing the money noise in order to find your true financial voice. During Week 3, we'll work on developing financial intimacy with our new financial voice through identifying financial beliefs and habits that align with our new way of thinking. During Week 4, we establish spiritual and tactical systems and structures to ensure that your new financial identity flourishes for the long haul.

Each daily teaching is accompanied by powerful lifework.

If you've read my other book, *The Happy Finances Challenge,* you'll be familiar with this feature. Lifework is an exercise or task I ask you to complete to unlock the mysteries of your relationship with money to give you clarity about the origins of your money feelings and decisions.

I've learned that the only way to close the gap between how you currently feel about money and how you want to feel is by being completely transparent and vulnerable with yourself throughout this process.

Even though I've built a strong financial foundation in my personal and business life over the last decade, I can honestly tell you that I've uncovered unexpected nuances to my financial identity as I worked through this book and completed the lifework.

A lot of us spend our youth chasing money, either spending it or hoarding it, only to realize we're in pursuit of the wrong thing. Don't get me wrong: we need money to meet many of our needs, and some of our wants; but once we use money to meet those needs and wants, we must look to and rely on our *relationship* with money to understand its limits.

Similar to modern theologian Reinhold Niebuhr's Serenity Prayer ("God, grant me the serenity to accept the things I cannot change, the courage to change the things I can, and the wisdom to know the difference") the quality of our relationship with money will give us the power to discern whether another dollar saved or trinket bought will truly get us closer to what we're looking for, which fundamentally boils down to feeling happy and safe and living with purpose and connection.

Love,

Kara

WEEK 1

We'll unpack our financial past in order to understand how it informs our current money identities.

Day 1: Connecting the Dots Between Money and Emotions

Even if we ignore sophisticated money algorithms, complicated spreadsheets, and the noise of the daily market watch, we intuitively know that a healthy handling of money comes when we mindfully save and mindfully spend.

That is, developing a healthy love and respect for money comes when we're able to strike a balance between saving and investing on the one hand and spending and philanthropy on the other. We know it makes sense to not only plan for retirement, but also enjoy our money on experiences, conveniences, and our guilty pleasures today.

So, if we logically understand this formula, why do we consistently fall short of the glory? What keeps our faces pressed to the proverbial glass, standing outside the pearly gates to the land of milk, honey, and happiness when it comes to our money?

The answer is simple: money is not logical. It's emotional.

Most of our money moves and decisions are rooted in the emotional chutney of our cultural upbringing, gender conditioning, socioeconomic status, media messaging, and familial and peer influences.

So if you never stopped to think about why you think what you think or believe what you believe about money, you'll have a passive and often unsatisfying relationship with your money and your money goals.

On the other hand, if you step back and begin to think about how emotions impact your ability to realize your desired financial goals, you'll be in a position of power and more likely to achieve them.

Today's lifework: Journal and/or free write your responses to any of the following prompts:
- What role have emotions played in your decision to overspend or oversave?
- Think about the current state of your finances. What role have your emotions played in creating this state?
- Since money decisions are emotional, are you feeling like a slave to your money emotions or the master of them?

Day 2: Write the Beginning Chapters of Your Money Story

I opened up this book by sharing my money story. I had little control over writing most of the chapters in that money story. Much of my money autobiography, ironically, starred my mother with me in a supporting role and reflected a money story characterized by unexamined beliefs and feelings I held about money for the first 30 years of my life.

But as I grew into financial wisdom, by seeing a therapist, eliminating massive amounts of debt (yet still feeling financial worry) and building The Frugal Feminista from the ground up, I learned how to keep the positive aspects of my former financial identity as a money hoarder and let go of those financial attributes that no longer served me or the financial goals I had set for myself as a grown and financially self-aware woman close to 40.

All of these experiences allowed me to reclaim the power of the pen. When you have the power of the pen, you can look at the financial identity that you currently embody as a function of the past and as merely a fraction of your full financial story, which you get to author on your own terms.

Today's lifework: Write the beginning chapters of your money story. Reference the money story I laid out in the introduction of this book as an example. Your money story can be as long or as short as you would like. As you write the beginning chapters of your money story, think about:

- Your earliest money memories from childhood
- Your most memorable money events in your adolescence
- Your most vivid experiences with money as an adult
- All of the feelings that accompanied these experiences

Bonus lifework: Scan your body after you've written this section of your money story. Write a poem, sketch an image, or call the first person that comes to mind to share what you're feeling and thinking.

Day 3: Give Your Money a Name and Give it a Voice

Yesterday, we took the time to think about your money story from childhood until now. You took the pen and wrote down the various memories and events as a way to notice and name the various instances that money was tied to a defining moment in your past.

Now we're going to deepen your awareness of money's influence on your life by personifying it. The irony about money is that, despite being an inanimate object, we assign so many human feelings or have such visceral responses to it: We love it, we fantasize about it, we kill over it, and we make sacrifices for it. But at the same time, many of us walk through life completely oblivious as to its power and influence.

So, when we personify money, we create a tangible entity, albeit fictional, to give you direct financial feedback about your money actions and moves.

Today's lifework: If money were a friend, what would she/he say behind your back in their journal? What nickname would money give you? What would this friend's feedback reveal about the quality of your relationship?

Here's an example from my money's diary. I call her Regina:

1/18/2012

Kara used to suffocate me. All she wanted to do was make more of me and look at me. All I did was sit in the bank account and grow and grow, but it never seemed to satisfy her. No matter how large I grew, she was always complaining that I wasn't enough. How ungrateful.

What's really hard to understand is that she never used me for the things she claimed she wanted to do like go shopping, go to plays, get her hair done. I hope she learns that she can keep me and do fun things with me. It's not one over the other.

If I had to give her a nickname it would be: Rich Kara, Poor Kara

What Regina's feedback taught me: *This type of journal entry would show that I haven't quite learned how to be thankful for the money I had and that I was stingy to myself and it was making me unhappy. And Regina showed me that tons of money didn't lead to contentment. There was something deeper preventing me from spending money on myself for pleasurable things.*

2/01/2018

I love being around Kara these days. She doesn't stress when a bill comes. She's not complaining about me not being enough. She saves me, she invests me, she splurges on her friends, her family, and herself (thank God for that.) Don't get me wrong, she still loves a good sale and she always places "paying herself first" at the top of her financial priorities, but she doesn't obsess about it. Is she perfect? Nah, but I can tell by how she makes her money decisions, it's not driven by fear or worry anymore. She's not so wrapped up in the limbs and branches, she's got a bigger financial vision and just seems more relaxed and confident about her ability to trust her money sense.

If I had to give her a nickname, it would be: Calm Kara

What Regina's feedback taught me: *This type of journal entry showed me that there's a chance for personal growth. We can all give ourselves second, third, and fourth chances. It also showed me that changing money behavior takes time, but is possible. And finally, I learned that my money beliefs were holding me back in so many other areas of my life.*

Now it's your turn.

Day 4: Create a Family Financial Geonogram aka Family Financial Family Tree

Lifework from Day 2 and Day 3 of *heal your relationship with money* helped us declutter and organize our current money emotions; in particular, we focused on how we feel about money and how our money "feels" about us. Essentially, we answered the question, "What are my money emotions?"

But for any deep money healing to occur, we also have to know the "why" and the "where" of our money emotions and beliefs. The good news is our current feelings and beliefs about money didn't occur in a vacuum. They are deeply rooted in our family of origins.

So, it will be our mission to tease out the specific messages we heard while growing up and see how *those* money beliefs and emotions contributed to forming our individual money thoughts.

For today's lifework: Jot down at least ten of the messages (spoken and unspoken) you received growing up about money. Also, write down who you learned that message from.

For example, if you saw your mother lie about how much she spent on clothes to your dad, you might have internalized the belief, "It's okay to lie about money in your marriage" or "Women have to answer to (and lie to) their men about spending money on themselves."

Money Message	Who Taught You This?

After doing this exercise, it's not uncommon to become awash with a number of strong, contradictory feelings. Many of my coaching clients shared that they felt resentful and relief at the same time: resentful because they were mad at their parents for not teaching them financial literacy and a deep sense of relief because they could finally understand *why* they spent the way they spent.

In general, they felt more in control because they could see - sometimes for the very first time - the cause-effect relationship between what they learned about money as a child with how they treated money as an adult.

Don't put this list away. We'll be using it tomorrow to generate even more financial clarity about who you are when it comes to money.

Day 5: Code and Categorize Your Money Messages

Yesterday, you wrote down the most salient money messages you heard, saw, and felt throughout your childhood and adolescence. When you place those messages under deeper scrutiny, you'll create a distance between you and those messages and emerge with a greater sense of objectivity and perspective.

For today's lifework, you'll evaluate and analyze your childhood money messages in two ways. First, you'll code the messages based on how positive, negative, or neutral the message was.

For example, when I was growing up, I learned never to trust men with money. I would classify that as "negative." On the other hand, my mother always had a side hustle and taught me the importance of using my creativity to make money, which was a positive and empowering money message.

Second, you'll code the money messages based on the message's bias. Some money messages have cultural, racial, gender, class, and religious bias. Sometimes one money message can contain several biases. Some messages, however, don't possess any of these biases. In this case, you can leave this column blank or place N/A for "not applicable."

For example, I was always raised with the belief that it was a woman's responsibility to care for her siblings no matter how old they were. I believe this money message is wrought with gender bias.

A belief like, *"Black women should just be happy to have a job and shouldn't complain about asking for promotions or more money"* contains cultural, racial and gender biases.

Money Message	Positive, Neutral, Negative	Cultural, Religious, Socioeconomic, Gender, or Racial Bias

We have one more piece of lifework to do with your deepest and ingrained money messages. Tomorrow's lifework will give you the power to fully detangle yourself from the part of your financial past that keeps you in cycles of financial dysfunction and disease.

Day 6: Draw Some Conclusions

We've been digging through the archives, clearing out the vault, airing our dirty laundry, and bringing what was in the darkness into the light -- whatever you want to call it. And like yesterday, you may still be in the midst of an emotional hangover: experiencing an unexpected emotional fatigue, a dogged determination to push through, or perhaps you're feeling unburdened for the first time in your life. And what's crazy is that you may be feeling all of these strong emotions all at the same time.

No worries, it's normal. This is happening because you've been intuitively drawing some conclusions about the quality of your money messages and you're ready to turn the proverbial corner on this chapter of your money life. But today, together, we are going to explicitly tally up the mental scorecard you've been keeping so you can be clear about what messages you'll carry into your new financial world and what messages you'll officially and ceremoniously part with by the end of tomorrow's lifework. **For today's lifework**: You are going to tally up the number of positive and negative money messages you received. After that, you're going to pay attention to what extent particular biases show up in these messages.

Money Message	Positive, Negative, Neutral	Bias at Play (i.e. cultural, religious, socio-economic, gender, racial, age)

Quality of Messages

How many empowering messages were you exposed to?

_____

How many disempowering messages were you exposed to?

_____

Were the majority of your money messages empowering or disempowering messages? How does that make you feel right now?

_____
_____
_____
_____
_____
_____

Nature of Money Messages

Reflecting on the nature of your money messages, is there a pattern with respect to bias? If so, which bias or biases have been prevalent in your money messaging?

_____
_____
_____
_____
_____
_____
_____

Day 7: Forgive with Compassion

I love Erykah Badu. One of my favorite songs is "Bag Lady" from her *Mama's Gun* album. In this song she encourages women to let go of whatever hurt and pain they have from the past so they can attract the love and joy they are looking for. In this song, she's referencing a man, but her advice about letting the pain and hurt go aptly applies to the people and experiences that soured your relationship with money.

If you listen to this song with a financial lens, it will empower you and give you the strength to leave your financial regrets and hurts behind.

The truth is your primary financial influences were doing the best they could with what they knew. And the other truth is *you* are doing the best you can with your finances with the tools and mindset that you have.

heal your relationship with money

By now, you've probably realized that there's a ton of room to grow. But to move forward with feelings of gratitude and compassion, we have to leave the past behind with some dignity and respect, not anger, bitterness, or rancor.

For today's lifework, you are going to make a list of people you want to forgive, including yourself and explain why you are forgiving them. (Play "Bag Lady" in the background to add an extra layer of support.)

My list would include my mother, my father, and myself. Here'll be my rationale for forgiveness:

- I forgive my mother for teaching me that the world was a dangerous and fearful place, full of people wanting to separate me from my money.
- My father is on the list for being the person to deeply hurt my mother and abandon my brother and me. It's hard, but I forgive him for leaving a big ol' gaping hole in our family.

- I forgive myself for being closed to love, ignoring my desires, and depriving myself of buying experiences and items that would add to my joy.

In my readings about forgiveness, I came across the Hawaiian Ho'oponopono prayer of forgiveness: *I'm sorry, please forgive me, thank you, I love you,* which you can use when you're forgiving yourself. Find a quiet place to do this prayer and say it over and over again. Consider placing your hand on your heart to fully commit to the words and the intentions.

Forgiveness List	Rationale for Forgiveness

Visit healyourrelationshipwithmoney.com/resources
to download the "I Am Worthy" worksheet.

WEEK 2

We'll focus on silencing the money noise in order to connect your true financial voice.

Day 8: Silence the Noise

During the first years of my marriage, my husband and I had some difficulty communicating about money. He grew up in a family where money wasn't a point of contention. They seemed to make do no matter how much money was coming in. In my home, however, money talks were largely negative and fear-based even when there was enough money to meet all of our needs and some of our wants.

Despite being a grown woman with a bucket load of degrees, a bank account, and a lot of job responsibilities, I was allowing my hurt and fearful seven-year-old self to call the shots in my marriage when it came to money.

For you it may not be your hurt seven-year-old self, but it may be your indulgent 10-year-old self that learned that financial boundaries are bad and wanting something is enough of a reason to acquire it. It may be your naive 16-year-old self that dreamed of being whisked away by an all-powerful man that would take care of you when you enter into a new relationship. Or one of the financial voices that speak on your behalf is a 32-year-old self that believes looking wealthy is more important than being wealthy and spends their whole paycheck on a bag or a pair of shoes.

Either way, these financial versions of yourself are not your true self. And sometimes we allow them to manage our money instead of our most evolved financial self.

For today's lifework, you're going to list all of the financial voices that reside in your head from the various junctures of your financial journey so you can silence them.

In addition to my hurt and fearful seven-year-old self, I'm going to add my 23-year-old people-pleasing self that gave away two of my most beautiful African pieces of fabric because I thought it would make that person my friend even though I knew deep down I would regret it.

Financial Voice	What They Do or Say to Impact Your Finances

Day 9: Build on the Strengths of Your Old Financial Identity

Yesterday we needed to take some time to sort out the various financial voices that clamor in our heads and clutter our thinking. Even though we said goodbye to all of the unhealthy financial beliefs and thinking we had inherited from the various influences in our lives, I have to share an idea that may seem to contradict all of the wonderful lifework we've done until now.

Here it is: No financial identity is 100% dysfunctional.

No matter how much financial shame and guilt they created, no matter how many relationships they have destroyed, and no matter how damaging our former financial identity was to our bottom line, each financial identity has some redeeming qualities which we can build on when we fully embrace our new financial voice.

For today's lifework, you're going to bring the benefits (no matter how small) to the surface. You'll complete the "Here's What I Already Bring to the Table" chart based on the strengths of your former financial identity.

Here's an example of what an oversaver may add:

Former Financial Identity: Penny Pincher
Here's What I Already Bring to the Table
- Strong sense of discipline
- Great researcher
- A large savings reserve

Here's an example of what an overspender may jot down:

Former Financial Identity: Baller, Shot Caller
Here's What I Already Bring to the Table
- Risk taker
- Generous to family members and others
- The ability to enjoy money

Now, you give it a chance.

Former Financial Identity:

_____

Here's What I Already Bring to the Table

-
-
-

Bonus lifework: Reflect on how you feel about this new way of perceiving your former financial identity.

Day 10: Embrace Your True Financial Voice or Alter Ego

Our true financial voice wants to make sure we are making the best decisions with our money at all times. And each of us has one if we sit long enough to listen and spend time soaking up her wisdom. But sometimes it's hard to hear her if you've never thought about her.

If it's a challenge for you to accept you have a true financial voice, consider embracing your financial alter ego. We all have an alter ego or secondary personality and today we are going to get to know her intimately.

When it comes to my finances, I have a financial voice, not necessarily an alter ego because I fully identify with my financial voice. Her name is my name and now we approach spending, saving, investing, and building a business from a balanced abundant perspective. She doesn't say no to pleasure purchases or experiences, but she makes sure her retirement, investments, and emergency funds are squared away. She's more open to taking on risk in business.

On the other hand, when it comes to my social life, I have an alter ego. She's a total extrovert. She is sassy, wears tight jumpsuits sans Spanx, and smacks on gum all day. All day. Her name is KK and I both love her and need her in my life. I ask her to come out when I'm ready for a turn-up or when I'm seeking adventure. I, however, insist she sit her little body down when it comes to speaking in front of large crowds, attending conferences, or when I'm asking for directions. I know her strengths and her weaknesses.

For today's lifework, you're going to name your financial voice or your financial alter ego, who will be your best financial self. Get to know her. Write down everything she says and does to show that she's speaking on your financial behalf.

My financial voice's or alter ego's name is:_____

I know she's my true financial voice or financial alter ego because she:

_____
_____
_____
_____
_____
_____
_____

What I love about my financial voice or my financial alter ego is:

_____
_____
_____
_____
_____
_____

Day 11: Listen to Your Financial Voice or Alter Ego

It's just not enough to briefly (re)acquaint yourself with your true financial voice or financial alter ego. It's time we clear head and heart space to hear what the woman's been trying to teach and tell you for years but couldn't because of all of the financial noise.

The positive messages you wrote down on Day 5 and Day 6 were just the fraction of her teachings she wants you to internalize.

For today's lifework, you're going to let her speak to you in two ways:

First, you're going to remix the negative money messages and make them empowering. If you had positive money messages from Day 5 and Day 6, add those too. It shows that your true financial voice was always there and, like I mentioned before, no financial identity is ever 100% toxic.

Second, you're going to brainstorm some of the new messages you want your true financial voice to remind you of more often.

Here's an example of life-saving teachings my financial voice has taught me:

Negative Money Message: Kara, spending is irresponsible so it should be avoided.

Remixed Money Message Courtesy of My True Financial Voice: Kara, spending doesn't make you irresponsible. Overspending does. You can spend on things you need and on things you want or desire as long as you've taken care of your financial responsibilities first.

Now it's your turn.

Negative Money Message	Remixed Money Message Courtesy of Your True Financial Voice

Day 12: Identify Your Core Values

Now that you've become acquainted with your financial voice or alter ego, we're going to actually rely on her to help you figure out what you really want to do with your money based on your core values.

Core values drive our behaviors and dictate what's most important to us at any given time in our lives. The irony is that many of us walk around unable to articulate what our core values are or what role they play in motivating us to make one money decision over the other. More often than not, we're parroting the core values of corporations and society at large.

Consequently, aligning your financial behaviors to your core values will make your spending and saving moves and decisions much more meaningful and deliberate. It's safe to conclude that when you're spending and saving behaviors are aligned to your personal truths, you tend to experience more fulfillment and joy in all areas of your life.

For today's lifework, we're going to help you identify your top ten core values. Below is a list of 57 common core values. Circle the values that resonate the most with you. (We'll be using this list tomorrow to help us align our spending to our values.) If you don't see a preferred core value, add it.

Here are four of mine.

>*Wealth*
>
>*Meaningful work*
>
>*Beauty*
>
>*Self-awareness* (I added this even though it wasn't on this list.)

Core Value List *(adapted from LeaderShape Institute)*

- Authenticity
- Achievement
- Adventure
- Authority
- Autonomy
- Balance
- Beauty
- Boldness
- Compassion
- Challenge
- Citizenship
- Community
- Competency
- Contribution
- Creativity
- Curiosity
- Determination
- Fairness
- Faith
- Fame
- Friendships
- Fun
- Growth
- Happiness
- Honesty
- Humor
- Influence
- Inner Harmony
- Justice
- Kindness
- Knowledge
- Leadership
- Learning
- Love
- Loyalty
- Meaningful Work
- Openness
- Optimism
- Peace
- Pleasure
- Poise
- Popularity
- Recognition
- Religion

- Reputation
- Respect
- Responsibility
- Security
- Self-Respect
- Service
- Spirituality
- Stability
- Success
- Status
- Trustworthiness
- Wealth
- Wisdom

Bonus lifework: How did you feel while completing this lifework? What new feelings or observations surfaced for you? What did you learn from them? Are the values you identified what you expected?

Day 13: Align Your Spending to Your Core Values

Understanding your core values is a necessary but not sufficient step toward aligning your spending to your values. Core values without actions (i.e. purchase of a material item, activity, or experience), attached to them are mere thoughts. Activities, items, and experiences allow your values to take root in the real world, especially when it comes to the decisions you make around money.

For today's lifework, you are going to pull out the list of ten values you compiled yesterday and attach one concrete activity, item, or experience that you do that aligns to this value. However, if you find that you haven't fully committed to spending or saving aligned to your values, fill out what you can and leave the rest, we'll work on that tomorrow.

Here's what my list would look like:

Core Value	Action Item
Wealth	Maxing out retirement contributions; growing The Frugal Feminista; saving over 30% of income.
Meaningful Work	Writing books, articles, and producing video content to help women heal their relationship with money.
Beauty	Indulging in monthly skin care treatments at a medical spa.
Self-awareness (not on the list)	Engaging in reflective practice all the time; taking time to read, write, journal, all to help me learn more about myself; buying a lot of books.

Now it's your turn.

Core Value	Action Item

Day 14: Close the Values Gap

Your money decisions will communicate the extent to which you are connecting with your money in real ways and show you how to better leverage money as a tool to help you bring more joy, peace, and lusciousness into your life.

That is, if you pay attention to how you spend and save.

If yesterday's lifework showed you that how you are using money now is not aligned to your core values, it's important to get clear about where your money *is* currently going.

For today's lifework, we'll do just that. With your most recent banking or credit card statements, use the "Where's My Money Really Going?" processing tool to help you get a handle on this. As an oversaver, this tool may help you see that you are investing and saving too much and not allowing yourself opportunities to spend based on your core values.

On the other hand, as an overspender, you may notice that your most recent debit card and/or credit card statement may reveal non-value based expenditure.

In particular, jot down any trends you notice. For example:

- Are you spending too much on clothes when your core value is adventure?
- Are you saving so much that you won't allow yourself to nurture your creative side which means spending a pretty penny on photography classes and equipment?

Where's My Money Really Going?

For the overspender, use this prompt:
I notice that I spend a lot of money on_____, when I really value _____ and should be spending my money on_____.

For the oversaver, use this prompt:

I notice that I spent little to nothing on _____when I really value_____. What I'm going to do differently is _____.

Bonus lifework: Apply the "Value/Don't Value It" rule:

Now that you're extremely clear about your values, it's time to put them to the test in order to assess whether your external environment reflects your internal money values. To ensure that what you already own and do will be in service to your new financial identity, think about applying the "Value / Don't Value It" rule to previous and future purchases.

For past and present money decisions:
- Go through each room of your home and determine if you value what you own. Whatever you don't value, pack it up and put it out - donate it to friends, charity, or family.

- Go through your calendar and see what activities you have lined up for yourself. Ensure that you have activities and experiences that align with your values. If not, add them. If you notice too many activities that don't align with your values, gracefully bow out if you can.

For future money decisions
- If you don't value it, then don't buy or do it. For overspenders, this limits buying for buying sake. For oversavers, it keeps you from buying the cheap or taking the hand-me-down (because it's free) instead of giving yourself permission to own your desires and your wants.

> Visit healyourrelationshipwithmoney.com/resources
> to download the "Pull the Trigger" journal prompt
> to further explore your money triggers.

WEEK 3

We'll focus on developing financial intimacy by identifying financial beliefs and habits that align with our new way of thinking.

Day 15: Track Your Spending and Saving the Right Way

There's a popular saying, "Whatever you pay the most attention to will grow." This dictum undergirds an all-important financial principle for both oversavers and overspenders, but not necessarily in a way most of us are taught to think.

Most financial advice around tracking money is about tracking how much you spend. Usually, this advice is directed to the overspender. But what most over-spenders do is...well, overspend, so tracking how much they've gone over budget is bound to make them avoid the process or feel so guilty about what they spent that they spend some more.

Similarly, when oversavers follow this advice, they may increase their sense of financial deprivation. Constantly paying attention to what they spend, outside the context of their overall wealth, may lead them to resort to tightening the proverbial belt unnecessarily and at the expense of their inner financial peace.

For today's lifework, we'll select how we are going to track our spending and saving in a way that makes sense for our financial identity.

For oversavers, it's important to track how much you spend in relation to your overall wealth. For example, if you spend 57 dollars on an impulse buy and you've done it a handful of times over the course of a few months or even one month, it's insignificant compared to an overall net worth of $200,000 in savings, retirement, or investing.

For the overspender, it's important for you to focus on your financial wins, no matter how small they are, when you're saving. Instead of tracking your spending, track your savings.

Consider using any of these to help you gain more financial perspective about your spending or saving patterns.

For overspenders:
- Set up text alerts for deposits over $5, $10, $15, etc. so you can see savings in real time.
- Set up weekly text alerts for your savings account so you can track how much your savings is growing incrementally.
- Create an Excel spreadsheet or use The Wealthy Woman's Blueprint Financial Planner to keep tabs on your money growth.

For oversavers:

- Set up text alerts for withdrawals over $100 dollars or any other number that makes sense to you. This way you won't engage in financial paranoia unnecessarily.
- Set up weekly text alerts so you can track the growth of your overall net worth.
- Create an Excel spreadsheet or use The Wealthy Woman's Blueprint Financial Planner to keep tabs on your money growth in relation to your spending.

Day 16: Name Your Bank Accounts

Names are powerful. Some cultures believe that what you name a child either speaks a life of blessings or curses onto their lives. Even though the case isn't so extreme with money, there's research that shows that connecting your money goals to a specific feeling will increase how committed you remain to achieving that goal.

Dr. Brad Klontz of the Financial Psychology Institute conducted a "Banking Reimagined" savings study to test whether positive memories attached to sentimental items could improve how Americans saved. Results from the study found that when positive feelings were activated, the emotional brain could visualize a goal and create concrete savings targets around it.

Participants named their bank accounts as part of this process. In naming their money destination, they were constantly reminded of their "why" or what they're working towards. Rather than focus on the sacrifice of saving (for the overspender) or spending (for the oversaver), the focus shifts to the financial reward.

I started this strategy a few years ago, without knowing the research behind it, and it keeps me excited and energized to spend as a chronic oversaver. Right now, I have one account I've named "Go to California with Regina Summer 2018." My girlfriend and I plan to stay for a week, which I'm estimating could run each of us at least $1,500. The name of the account helps me focus on the foolishness and trouble we plan to get into, the bond we'll strengthen, the memories we'll make, the food we'll eat, and the lessons we'll share rather than the $1,500 I'd save if I didn't go.

On the other hand, if you're struggling with spending, but one of your deepest desires is to own your home or quit your job, naming your accounts "Downpayment for My Slice of the American Pie 2021" or "Be My Own Boss 2022" will get you motivated and focused on your spending. Rather than view the newest tech or gel mani-pedi Groupon as worthwhile, you know they'll never compare to the feelings of pride and confidence you'll feel when you receive the keys to your home or tender your resignation.

For today's lifework, you're going to name your bank accounts. (If your bank doesn't allow you to name them, consider online banks like Ally or Capital One 360 that do). When you name your bank account(s), create a vivid description that speaks to your desired financial outcome and a deadline.

Bank Account Name #1 _____

Why is this goal more important than oversaving or overspending?

_____

_____

_____

_____

_____

Bank Account Name #2 _____

Why is this goal more important than oversaving or overspending?

_____

_____

_____

_____

_____

Bank Account Name #3 _____

Why is this goal more important than oversaving or overspending?

_____

_____

_____

_____

_____

Day 17: Schedule Dates with Your Money

If you're a social butterfly, you keep your social calendar booked. If you're obsessed with make-up and fashion, I'm certain you make time to get your hair and nails "did." If you want to work on building your relationship with your partner or you're looking for one, it's a given that you'll make time to date your spouse or attend events that will help you find love. Finally, if you're a gym rat, you consider the time you carve out for CrossFit, yoga, running, or strength training sacred and non-negotiable.

The same goes for making time to get intimate with your money. In order to learn how to care for it so it will care for you, you have to make it a priority. And you make things a priority when you consistently carve out time for them.

For today's lifework, you're going to take out your digital or physical calendar to schedule money dates to:

- Organize your files
- Check credit score
- Send in rebates and deductibles
- Review your investments
- Convert loose change into dollars
- Pay credit card bills
- Consolidate student loans
- Automate abundance (See Day 21 for more on this)
- Establish your FFF (See Day 20 for more on this)
- Calculate your net worth
- Speak to human resources about your retirement allocations
- Listen to a podcast
- Create a soulful saving or spending plan (See Day 13 for more on this)

heal your relationship with money

This list is by no means exhaustive but will get you thinking about ways to connect with your money in a consistent, action-oriented way.

Focus of "Money Date"	Date and Time for "Money Date"

To keep you from feeling overwhelmed, consider starting small, with one or two money dates a month.

Day 18 : Assemble Your Money Squad

Behind every financially healed woman is a crew of supporters guiding and cheering her on. You will have to pay for some of them to be a member of your money squad, and some of them you'll acquire organically. And usually, you should aim for three levels of support in your money squad.

Level 1: Money Mentors

Money mentors include money professionals and experts. They know more than you and can give you specific information or guidance on your money journey. Here are some money mentors you may want to include in your money squad:

- **An accountant** prepares and examines financial records. Accountants make sure records are accurate and that taxes are paid properly and on time.
- **A personal finance coach** can help you create a soulful spending plan (aka budget), help you identify money blocks and financial trig-

gers, and keep you accountable as you reach your financial goals.
- **A financial advisor** analyzes your current financial situation, learns what your goals are, and creates a plan in order for you to meet these goals. Financial advisors focus on the long game—retirement, education savings, and estate planning.

Level 2: Money Amigas

Money Amigas are members of your money squad who are at similar stages of their money journey. You can find them in paid and free online communities via platforms like Facebook or Meetup. Facebook groups like my Heal Your Relationship with Money Community or Dream Catchers run by my financial friend Tiffany Aliche are two great places to start.

You can also find Money Amigas in your social circles. These women are girlfriends who are tired of living in financial dysfunction and are open to being an accountability partner, a sounding board, and a truth-teller.

The great thing about Money Amigas is that you already have a friendship. As a Money Amiga, you'll have *another* dimension of connection and compatibility.

Level 3: Money Mentees

Money mentees are the women of your money squad who need your financial guidance and encouragement. Money mentees aren't necessarily younger than you; they are women at the beginning of their financial journey and you'll be there to share your story and share resources.

The process of money mentoring or teaching helps reinforce the money lessons you've learned over the course of your journey. Plus, you get the added benefit that you've made the world a less financially dysfunctional place.

For today's lifework, you're going to assemble your money squad. You'll determine who you already have in your money squad and who's missing from it.

Who Do I Have Already?

Money Mentor	Money Amigas	Money Mentees

Who's Missing from My Money Squad?

Money Mentor	Money Amigas	Money Mentees

Once you have a clear understanding of where you stand with your money squad, be sure to communicate with them for a meeting or conversation within the next 48 hours. Consider sending emails to your money mentors and texts or phone calls to your Money Amigas or money mentees.

Day 19 : Build Your Money Library

I remember the day I started to get my financial life together like it was yesterday. I had opened up a Discover Card bill only to find out that my balance had increased due to a late payment penalty. In my naive, miserly mind, I thought, "Why do they keep sending me these bills? It's not like I'm going to pay them back." I believed that if I avoided payments long enough, the credit card (and student loan) companies would get tired of asking me for the money and move on with their lives.

My mom was standing there as I opened the bill and looked at me screw faced (because she believed she had taught me better) and asked something to the effect, "Well, what are you going to do about it?"

I looked back at her and wondered, "Yeah, what am I going to do?" sincerely puzzled by the whole situation.

heal your relationship with money

A voice inside of me (my true financial voice) said, "Go to the library."

It all clicked. Even though I was a financial hot mess, I was always a good student and the strategy of reading made sense to me. Reading was a surefire way to teach me about money. It wasn't long before I went to my local library and asked the librarian about books about money. She sent me to the personal finance section and Glinda Bridgforth's *Girl, Get Your Money Straight* jumped right out to me. This book was everything I needed and more, and without me realizing it, planted the seed to build a career in helping women like me get their money worlds right side up.

Now, reading books may not be your choice of support, but books aren't the only way to build your money "library." Here are a few more:

- Articles and blogs provide short-form money guidance and information.
- Podcasts allow you to listen to money advice from your favorite money friends and thought

leaders. A few of my favorites are the Redefining Wealth podcast by Patrice Washington, Happy Black Woman by Rosetta Thurman, and Prosperity Place by Joan Sotkin.

- Conferences can range from a few hours to a few days, depending on the length of the event. You'll be able to hear various money gurus speak about money with like-minded people.
- Retreats allow you to delve into money topics in a more intimate setting, usually in a remote locale.

For today's lifework, you'll make a list of the best ways to stock your money "library" and begin to think about setting aside a budget for the higher-priced opportunities.

Day 20 : Be a Coin Collector

When you begin to heal your relationship with money, you'll start to shift your thinking and begin to see that there's enough money to go around for you both to spend and save, without feeling deprived. One of the best places to start practicing this mindset is by how you treat your loose change.

A lot of us overlook loose change and don't give it the respect it deserves. But it's money. It's money that you could use as the building blocks of your savings account or money to fund a splurge.

For today's lifework, you're going to begin (or re-commit) to your Financial Freedom Fund (FFF) or loose change bucket, jar, or basket. I coined this term (no pun intended) to show my clients the power of persistence and baby steps.

Here are 6 steps to create your own FFF.

1. Find the right container for your FFF. The size of your FFF will dictate how long it'll take you to fill it. So, if you're looking for a quick win, start with a smaller FFF.
2. Decorate it (optional). Decorate your FFF with vibrant colors, images, and words especially if the act of beautifying it will inspire you to fill it up.
3. Establish the purpose of the FFF. If you're an overspender, you can use this money for guilt-free spending that's not attached to your monthly budget. As an overspender, you could also use your FFF as a reminder to save. If you're an oversaver, you could use this money like an overspender for guilt-free spending. This money won't interfere with your monthly savings goals.
4. Throw all of your loose change in there at the end of each day. If you live in a house, have a few FFFs around high traffic areas such as

kitchens and bedrooms. When necessary, combine all of the money into the central FFF.
5. Redeem your coins for cash.
6. Spend or save without guilt or deprivation (see Step 3 to reinforce your spending or saving rationale).

Day 21 : Automate Abundance

Healing your relationship with money is fundamentally a conversation about making an abundance mindset the basis of your financial thinking. A practical financial structure of an abundance mindset is the idea of paying yourself first.

When you pay yourself first, you route your specified savings or (spending contribution) from each paycheck at the time it is received.

But this concept of paying yourself first often falls short with a busy schedule and when your old money thinking clouds your true financial desires.

The best way to make sure you consistently meet your weekly or monthly spending or savings goals is to ensure that you automate them.

When you automate your abundance, whether it be spending goals as an oversaver or your savings goals as an overspender, you'll never miss a beat.

For today's lifework, you're going to pull out your calendar and schedule a time that you're going to automate your savings. If you're not the most tech savvy, you're going to schedule a time to call customer service to walk you through the process. Make sure you schedule the automation of your abundance in the next 48 hours.

Mission: Automate Abundance

Date: _____

Time: _____

Visit healyourrelationshipwithmoney.com/resources to download money templates to download the "Saving with Soul" template to help you set intentional savings goals.

WEEK 4

We'll establish spiritual and tactical systems and structure to ensure that your new financial identity flourishes for the long haul.

Day 22 : Notice and Name Your Financial Triggers

Even the most financially savvy person has their financial triggers. When you hear the term "financial trigger", you usually hear it in the con-text of experiences, like pulling out the credit card when you're having a bad day to make you feel better. But financial triggers aren't limited to that. Certain places, times of year, times of day, and individuals can trigger you, making it easy for your old (and less evolved) financial self to make money decisions.

In many instances, however, we aren't even aware of our triggers, so we react rather than respond to them.

For today's lifework, we are going to take back our financial control and name our financial triggers on three levels: with experiences, people, and places. Think about the last five instances where you were financially triggered and how it impacted your money moves.

Here a few examples to help guide your individual work taking into account potential triggers for over-savers and overspenders:.

Instance	Financial Feeling	Type of Financial Trigger	Which part of your financial identity is making this decision?
Going shopping more than two days in a row or spending more than $100 at a time	Losing control	Experience	Fearful child self
Spending behind partner's back	Vindictive and powerless	Conversation with partner	Rebellious 20-something self
Going into debt to book the most ex-	Entitlement; need for adoration	Time of year	Competitive 30-year old self

pensive suite for 30th bday			
Scrolling through Amazon late at night	Boredom	Time of day	Lonely teenage self
Buying an (unnecessary) expensive e-course at a conference after conference leader pitches it	Enthusiasm + Fear of Missing Out (FOMO)	Experience	Gullible teenage self
Buying an item after you saw a post on social media	Envy	Experience	Competitive teenage self

Now it's your turn.

Instance	Financial Feeling	Type of Financial Trigger	Which part of your financial identity is making this decision?

Day 23 : Have a Game Plan for Your Financial Triggers

Yesterday, we engaged in a deep dive of our financial triggers to give us some important information about our financial vulnerability. The goal is not to eliminate our financial vulnerabilities or avoid them. The beauty of having a healthy relationship with money is that we know we don't have to be perfect and void of financial frailties. The power of financial self-awareness gives us the power to manage our triggers in a way that keeps us aligned with our new beliefs and values.

For today's lifework, we are going to create a plan of preemptive support to minimize the intensity, length, and impact of our financial triggers. Go back to the list of financial triggers you listed and create enriching and proactive responses.

Take a look at my plan to give you some ideas.

Financial Trigger	What's a Healthier Response?
Going shopping more than two days in a row or spending more than $100 at a time	Using positive self-talk that places purchases in perspective Paying in cash Spacing out buying
Spending behind partner's back	Communicating about the purchase Establishing a dollar amount that doesn't require consensus with partner Opting to not buy the item
Going into debt to book the most expensive suite for 30th bday	Planning for birthday in advance Finding a different place Paying in cash

Scrolling through Amazon late at night	Reading a book instead Establishing a 48-hour "cool off" period before purchasing Abandoning sales cart
Buying an (unnecessary) expensive e-course at a conference after conference leader pitches it	Leaving the room when the pitch is made Using positive self-talk about having enough

Now it's your turn.

Financial Trigger	What's a Healthier Response?

Day 24: Scrutinize Your Money Self-Talk

Changing your money thinking is a recursive process. It's like trying to tip over a vending machine: it doesn't happen in one shot. So, it's not uncommon to fall back into negative or dysfunctional money talk, especially when you're stressed at home or work. To make room for your new financial thoughts to build strong roots, you have to create a process or practice to help you move forward. I've used these three steps to help pivot my thinking when I'm spiraling into the world of scarcity.

1. Question the validity of your old money thought. For example, if you say, "Ohhh! I like that dress, so I'm going to buy it. Besides, you only live once," you can ask yourself: "How true is this statement? Do I have to buy everything I like? Does "living only once" mean I break my budget or use my emergency fund money on something I like?"

2. Assess how old money thinking will impact the new way you want to think about money.

How does thinking "I buy what I want when I want it" support the new money belief of "I can buy some things I want, but it's not necessary to buy everything I want because I have bigger goals"?

3. Think about how your new money belief will change your life. A belief like, "I can buy some things I want, but it's not necessary to buy everything I want because I have bigger goals" can help me both enjoy my money now while simultaneously saving for the future. This new money belief is a win-win.

For today's lifework, you're going to think about three old money messages that spring up when you're stressed and go through this three-part process.

heal your relationship with money

Old Money
Mesage#1 _____
_____
_____

Answers:

Step 1:
_____
_____
_____
_____

Step 2:
_____
_____
_____
_____

Step 3:
_____
_____
_____
_____
_____

Old Money

Mesage#2_____

_____

_____

_____

Answers:

Step 1:

_____

_____

_____

_____

Step 2:

_____

_____

_____

_____

Step 3:

_____

_____

_____

_____

_____

heal your relationship with money

Old Money
Mesage#3 _____

_____
_____
_____

Answers:

Step 1:

_____
_____
_____
_____

Step 2:

_____
_____
_____
_____

Step 3:

_____
_____
_____
_____
_____

Day 25 : Create a Beautiful Money Space

My mom was a glossy pet when I was growing up. That's our affectionate term for a woman that loved glamour and girly stuff. Makeup did. Hair did. Perfume on. Heels stacked.

And she always chewed Trident discreetly to keep the breath minty fresh.

My mom was *that* Monday through Friday.

But on the weekend and especially on bill paying Sunday, she looked completely different. She wore a tattered housecoat, crooked glasses, and sat at the dining table looking distraught. Bills, papers, and envelopes were strewn across the table and from my kid eyes, she looked like she was drowning.

Memories like these left a financial imprint that messaged that handling money was an ugly, unpleasant experience, literally.

heal your relationship with money

And it goes to show that one's physical environment can reflect what's going on inside.

And it took me years of reflection to reverse this thinking and I'll be damned if I let you show up to your finances in the same way.

So, for **today's lifework,** we are going to set up a money space that invites positive feelings and positive thoughts. Here's how:

1. Find a space that will only be for you to handle your money. It could be your desk, a corner in your bedroom, or in your home office.

2. Declutter this space. Don't use this space for anything other than caring for your money.

3. Organize this space. Depending on your needs, you may want a few supplies like (pretty) pens, Post-its, and folders. It's also a good idea to keep your computer in this space if you do a lot of your banking online. But don't overdo it.

You want to keep the space clean and with minimal clutter.

4. Decorate the space. To uplevel the spiritual and emotional energy of the space, consider placing a vision board (if you respond to visuals), candles, or even pictures of your money inspirations (i.e. your family, your friends, or a picture of a happy you.)

Day 26: Create "Invitation-Only" Statements

Our minds are readily equipped to accept the critical unsavory things we say about ourselves and our money as truth. Luckily, it's equally prepared to instantly accept any positive affirming words we speak over our lives.

If we're willing to work at it...

That's where the power of affirmations come in. Affirmations are what I like to call "invitation-only words." They are the statements that we purposefully create and construct in support of us reaching our biggest goals. In the case of finances, money affirmations will help us develop uplifting and nurturing beliefs about our abilities to reach our desired financial goals and outcomes.

You'll see a variety of ways to create an affirmation and they all can work. What's most important is that you can see yourself believing the statement. Here are some guidelines for creating money affirmations that make sense for you.

Keep it positive. At the time of this book, I've been working on my beliefs about being heard and seen. I want to feel more comfortable about taking up more space in this world and in my finances. So, an appropriate financial affirmation could be "It's safe for me to take up space" or "It's safe for me to be seen" or "It's safe for me to have my needs met."

Start your affirmations with "I" or "My" if you can. The affirmations I listed above didn't start with "I" or "My" but they are still powerful (to me). When constructing your affirmation, consider starting with phrases like "I can" or "I am."

Keep your affirmations short. When your affirmations are short, they are easier to remember.

Keep it in the present. When you write your affirmations as if you're experiencing them now, you show up for that statement now, not in the future.

Add emotions to your affirmations. Phrases like "I am [emotion] about . . ." or "I feel [emotion] about [goal, desire]" connect the action to the feeling.

Create affirmations that you believe. If you write an affirmation that is virtually impossible for you to believe now, write another one that starts with, "I am open to [desired goal, feeling, outcome] . . ." or "I am willing to believe I could [desired outcome] . . ." You'll be able to eliminate the qualifier the more confident you become.

Replace your affirmations as needed. There's no time limit on how long you should meditate on a particular affirmation.

For an overspender, a financial affirmation may sound like, "I can save 10% of my income every month with ease and grace. Saving is important to me."

For an oversaver, an affirming financial affirmation may sound like, "I can afford to buy things I love without guilt or remorse. I am worth it."

For today's lifework, you're going to brainstorm 10-15 affirmations and choose three that resonate the most for you.

1.
2.
3.
4.
5.
6.
7.
8.
9.
10.

11.

12.

13.

14.

15.

Bonus lifework: Create a schedule for using your financial affirmations. Here's a quick planning guide for your money affirmation practice:

- Which days of the week will you engage in your money affirmation practice?
- Will you repeat them once a day or several times a day?
- Will you do it alone or with someone?
- Will you write your affirmations down?

Here's an example of my practice to give you an idea of what you could do.

I use the first five minutes of every day to engage in money affirmations at my desk at work in addition to listening to my favorite podcasts.

I also use my affirmation, "It's safe to take up space" when I'm about to send a follow-up email to a company that I want to work with or when I feel I'm about to enter a meeting where I have to advocate for myself. I normally don't write my money affirmations down because I journal, though I think it's a great strategy.

Day 27 : Become a Boss at Spotting EF Money

One of the biggest telltale signs of a healthy relationship with money is when you're able to spot and appreciate EF money, or effortlessly free money, no matter the amount.

EF money is extra money that comes to you without a lick of hard work. EF money means you click a button, fill out a form, spend an extra hour or two at work, or share a resource. But it never comes from activities that will have you stressed out, pushing and pulling, hustling or grinding.

You can save the EF or spend the EF. If the EF is a large amount, as an overspender or oversaver, you could allocate a percentage to spend or a percentage to save. Start at a 50-50 save/spend split and work your way up or down the percentage.

For today's lifework, you're going identify some EFs with which you're already familiar and make a note of some that you want to bring into your financial life.

- Insurance claims
- Money on the street
- Money in your old purses, couch, pockets
- Gift cards
- Coupons
- Referrals (if you're in business)
- Favors from friends and family that save you money or in-kind donations
- Rewards points on your credit cards
- Paid overtime for something you're already doing
- Affiliate links for making genuine recommendations to friends and family
- Gifted courses and classes
- Credits on utility bills
- Work bonuses and raises
- Tax refunds
- Money from class action suits
- Sign up bonuses at banks or credits to sites you had plans to use already
- Inheritance

Bonus lifework: Pick a way to demonstrate your gratitude. Here are a few ways to get your EF-gratitude juices flowing:

- Happy dancing
- Praise dancing
- A quiet or loud high five to the Universe
- A prayer
- Paying it forward by doing something nice for someone else
- A soul clap
- Lighting a candle
- Marking the date and the amount on your calendar

Day 28: Decide to be Enough Now

A lot of us use money to measure significance: how much space we can readily take up in this world, and on whom to project feelings of adoration and envy. We live in a celebrity-worship society so it's not hard to feel like our lives don't stack up against the conspicuous displays of wealth, importance, and power.

If you're an overspender, you may try to keep up by spending like you have a million in the bank. If you're an oversaver, you may try to demonstrate your power by attempting to squirrel away a million.

But it's important to understand this spiritual principle: You're worthy independent of what you buy and don't buy, independent of how much you have stacked in the bank or don't have stacked in the bank. If you never bought another handbag, plane ticket or lakefront home, you'll still be enough to those who matter to you the most.

Similarly, if you never saved another red cent or generated another stream of income, you'll still be enough.

For our final lifework together, you're going to meditate on this principle and think about what this principle would actually look like in practice tomorrow and the rest of your life. The truth is that we all cognitively know that we are enough, but our words and actions don't always align.

Jot down five ways you're going to demonstrate you're enough right now.

For example, an overspender may decide to not to buy another dress this month because she understands that another dress isn't going to change how people will perceive her.

On the other hand, an oversaver may decide not to stay at work for the extra overtime and go to the gym, read a book, or spend time with family instead.

I know I'm enough. This is how I'll show it through my spending and saving habits immediately by:

1.

2.

3.

4.

5.

> Visit healyourrelationshipwithmoney.com/resources to download money templates to download the "Understand Your Numbers" template to help your new financial identity flourish.

A Final Note about Your Money Story

"The only thing that's keeping you from getting what you want is the story you keep telling yourself about why you can't have it." – Tony Robbins

When I was a little girl, I would spend hours on my bed writing short stories and fiery brown girl poetry and prose before I ever heard the word "feminist" or "womanist." I was convinced I was going to be a fiction writer and tell nuanced, complex, and messy stories about Black women's humanity like my favorite literary aunties Jamaica Kincaid and Alice Walker.

But then I discovered the world of personal finance in my mid-twenties and fell hard. Up until this time fiction had been my one and only tenderoni, giving me a chance to explore and expand my understanding of the world and myself through the characters I had created. Personal finance, however, eliminated the need for me to make up a character or an alternate world in order to forge an intimate relationship with myself.

I eventually created The Frugal Feminista to make it safe for all of us to share our stories. Whether through the books I write, the courses I create, the keynote speeches I give, or the one-on-one coaching I provide, it's an honor for me to secure space for women to share our money stories, rewrite our stories, and reinvent how we see ourselves along the way.

We no longer have to blame our parents or society for the financial influences they made on our lives because we now hold the pen and hold the power to construct the stories we've always wanted to not merely hear, but also believe about ourselves, our worth, and our magic.

Writing *heal your relationship with money* was as much for me as it was for you. This book, of all of the books I've written, has empowered me to be more compassionate with myself as I move and stumble through life, set new goals, and create new intentions with the ideas and dreams I give my permission to entertain and pursue.

It's my hope that this book has equipped you with the right balance of money knowledge and money wisdom to take full responsibility for the next chapter you'll write in your money narrative.

Love always,

Kara

P.S. Don't be a stranger. I love hearing how your relationship with money has changed for the better. Share your money stories with me on social media:

Instagram: @FrugalFeminista
Facebook: The Frugal Feminista
Twitter: @FrugalFeminista
Email: kara@thefrugalfeminista.com

ABOUT THE AUTHOR

Kara Stevens is an author, speaker, and founder of The Frugal Feminista, a personal finance and personal development company committed to helping women live life on their own terms unapologetically. She is also the creator of The Financial Fullness Framework, a trauma-informed curriculum to help BIPOC communities heal their relationship with money so they can grow wealth and release money guilt, shame, worry, and fear.

After climbing her way out of $65K worth of student loan and credit card debt, building up her financial reserves, and aggressively investing in equities, Kara soon saw the link between personal power and financial freedom and wanted to inspire and educate other women around the world about increasing their financial acumen and self-confidence.

A teacher, historian, connector, and activist at heart, Kara wants to lead a "Frugal Feminista" revolution – to change the conversation between girlfriends, between husbands and wives, and between mothers and daughters about money.

Kara is a native New Yorker and first-generation American via the beautiful island of Antigua. She possesses a BA in Political Science from Oberlin College, a MSEd in Bilingual Education from CUNY's Hunter College and an EdM in Organizational Leadership from Columbia University's Teachers College.

She lives between Ghana, West Africa and New York City where she enjoys spending time with her husband and daughter.

LET'S STAY CONNECTED

Join Heal Your Relationship with Money Community, my free financial safe space on Facebook, to receive encouragement, inspiration, resources, and support on your financial journey.

For all speaking invitations, media requests, and PR inquiries, email me at kara@thefrugalfeminista.

Printed in Great Britain
by Amazon